ARLINGTON NATIONAL CEMETERY

A NATION'S STORY CARVED IN STONE

ARLINGTON NATIONAL CEMETERY

A NATION'S STORY CARVED IN STONE

PHOTOGRAPHS BY LORRAINE JACYNO DIETERLE
World War II Coast Guard SPAR

FOREWORD BY SENATOR JOHN MCCAIN
Captain, United States Navy, Retired

Military Women's Press

Pomegranate
SAN FRANCISCO

*To my beloved husband Walter, who taught me to take time to think before I clicked
that shutter, and to my sister, June Droz, whose support I will always treasure.*

Published by Pomegranate Communications, Inc.
Box 6099, Rohnert Park, California 94927
1-800-277-1428; www.pomegranate.com

Pomegranate Europe Ltd.
Fullbridge House, Fullbridge
Maldon, Essex CM9 4LE, England
(44) 1621 851646

Library of Congress Cataloging-in-Publication Data

Dieterle, Lorraine Jacyno.
    Arlington National Cemetery : a nation's story carved in stone / photographs by Lorraine Jacyno Dieterle.
        p. cm.
    Includes index.
    ISBN 0-7649-1742-0
    1. Arlington National Cemetery (Arlington, Va.)—History—Pictorial works. 2.
Arlington National Cemetery (Arlington, Va.)—Pictorial works. I. Title.

    F234.A7 D54 2001
    975.5'295—dc21   2001032113

Pomegranate Catalog No. A615
ISBN 0-7649-1742-0

Cover and interior design by Laura Lind Design, Fort Bragg, California

Printed in Korea

10 09 08 07 06 05 04 03   10 9 8 7 6 5 4 3

CONTENTS

Foreword *by Senator John McCain,*
Captain, United States Navy, Retired 6

Preface *by Lorraine Jacyno Dieterle,*
World War II Coast Guard SPAR 7

Acknowledgments 8

Biography 8

Introduction *by Linda Witt, Women In Military*
Service For America Memorial Foundation, Inc. 9

Map of Arlington National Cemetery 14–15

Points of Interest .15

Memorial Day 16

Tomb of the Unknowns 20

The Eternal Flame .28

Processions 32

Women at Arlington 38

African Americans in the Civil War 44

Memorials 46

Notable Stones 62

Arlington Through the Seasons 72

Index 93

FOREWORD

Arlington, our nation's preeminent national cemetery, gracefully and silently honors the men and women who served in the armed forces.

In the past few years, we have witnessed a resurgence of interest in what popularly has been called the last great war: World War II. Films like *Saving Private Ryan* and books like Tom Brokaw's *The Greatest Generation* and James Bradley and Ron Power's *Flags of Our Fathers* poignantly remind us of a period when the United States mobilized like at no other time in its history and, during a moment of great violence and terror, demonstrated the courage with which the "greatest generation" came of age.

My grandfather was a naval aviator, my father a submariner. They were my first heroes. Both have come to be buried here. I remember visiting the graves of my grandfather and father one cold, snowy day in Arlington National Cemetery. I walked along the white-blanketed road, free of any footprints but mine, and looked out across the rows and rows of nearly identical headstones solemnly jutting up from the ground like magnificent trees in a ghostly orchard. I had thought that the simple, white headstones would be camouflaged by the snow as it fell and collected on the ground. But no, each stone—as each sacrifice it represented—stood out.

As I walked down the hill, I continued to reflect. I have memories of a place, Vietnam, so far removed from the comforts of this blessed country, yet I have forgotten some of the anguish it once brought me. But my happiness here these past three decades has not let me forget the friends who did not come home with me. The memory of them, of what they bore for honor and country, causes me to look hard at every prospective conflict for the shadow of Vietnam.

These headstones span many wars and many generations of young Americans, all different and yet all alike, like the markers above their graves. Most of the young Americans who rest here did not garner military honors like the well-decorated Audie Murphy, yet they are all deserving of our most sincere respect.

The world in which our servicemen and servicewomen shoulder their responsibilities is an uncertain one. Our familiarity with man's inhumanity to man assures us that Americans will be asked someday to again bear sacrifices that only the bravest can endure. That burden will be their honor, as it once was mine. My memories of that honor remain vivid. The willingness of some to give their lives so that others may live in freedom never fails to evoke in us a sense of wonder, mystery, and admiration. I pray that if the time comes for more young Americans— our blood and our treasure—to answer a call to arms, the battle will be necessary and the field well chosen.

I know that on some fitting, distant occasion, young men and women will be instructed in their duty by recalling the example of those who went before them. And on a quiet bench somewhere, many years from now, the liberated will again gather to pay tribute to the liberators, look upon their seasoned faces, and say: They were warriors once and very brave. I understand how great an honor that is.

—Senator John McCain
Captain, United States Navy, Retired

PREFACE

I n the summer of 1998, I watched the flag-draped coffin of a dear friend and fellow veteran being lowered into her grave at Arlington National Cemetery. As I listened to the haunting notes of "Taps," my mind raced back half a century to World War II and my own service as a photographer in the United States Coast Guard. Remembering the men and women with whom I had served, I thought of those who never returned. I recalled the combat photographers I trained, who went on to cover the landings at Omaha and Utah Beaches in Normandy and at Guadalcanal in the Pacific. I remember the horror and carnage captured in the photographs they sent back, which I had to inspect before releasing to the public. Fifty years ago I had vowed that I would keep alive the memory of all veterans.

After my friend's interment, I returned to the cemetery and walked for hours among the graves of the many brave men and women. I saw the markers of men who fought in the Civil War, of nurses who treated the wounded of the Spanish-American War, of Medal of Honor recipients, of men and women who had served both in war and peace from the American Revolution to the present day. I knew then that I could fulfill my wartime promise by presenting this national memorial with respect, honor, and dignity. I want every American of every generation to remember the sacrifices their nation's veterans made to preserve freedom for all time.

—Lorraine Jacyno Dieterle
World War II Coast Guard SPAR

ACKNOWLEDGMENTS

To Arlington National Cemetery Superintendent John C. Metzler Jr. and Historian Tom Sherlock, for their assistance and support; Brigadier General Wilma L. Vaught, USAF, Retired, and president of the Women In Military Service For America Memorial Foundation, for her repeated affirmation that "Women are veterans, too"; my editor, Linda Witt, for guidance, expertise, and just the right "push"; Yvonne Brown and Robert Brown, whose help in locating specific stones and memorials was invaluable; John H. Doung, for superb photoprocessing; my sons Colonel Kurt Dieterle, USMC, Retired, Annapolis '70 and former U.S. Army Captain Mark Dieterle, West Point '73, my daughters-in-law Carol and Elaine, and my grandsons Jeffrey, Brian, and Matthew, whose love gave me the courage to tackle this project; and especially to Donna Houle, for starting me on this incredibly rewarding endeavor—thank you all!

To the United States Coast Guard and my sister SPARs: when our country called we were ready. Semper Paratus!

BIOGRAPHY

In World War II Lorraine Jacyno Dieterle served in the United States Coast Guard as a SPAR (the acronym for Coast Guard women) in the Third Naval District, headquartered in New York City. She taught combat and aerial photography to GI photographers who would soon see action and then inspected and cataloged their war zone photographs, weeding out those too graphic for release to newspapers and the public. After the war, she was a professional photographer and animator for major corporations, including Bell and Howell, and married Walter Dieterle, another World War II veteran, who died in 1994. Dieterle resides in Virginia and is Director of Volunteers and Staff Photographer for the Women In Military Service For America Memorial at Arlington National Cemetery.

INTRODUCTION

The stones tell America's story. Row after row of nearly identical marble headstones climb gentle Virginia hills and stand in mute testimony to fallen heroes and heroines. Even at a distance—from the air or from the river of traffic streaming along the George Washington Parkway beside the Potomac River—the meaning of the stones is clear. Men and women died to create this country; other men and women rammed cannon, shouldered guns, or piloted jet fighters to secure liberty. We have known these warriors century after century, generation after generation, war after war. Here, we meet them row after row.

Once brother took up arms against brother and slaves fought masters; now all are resting here. A mother and daughter, both nurses in the Spanish-American War, shared a life of nurture and now have a common tombstone here. Soldiers of the Revolutionary War and sailors of the War of 1812, the Civil War's often nameless U.S.C.T. ("Colored Troops") and World War II's Tuskegee Airmen, presidents and poor men, the famous and the Unknowns, generals and admirals and buck privates: all are honored here. Their individual stones join others that recall battles and battalions or list those who died in one stunning moment—on the Space Shuttle *Challenger,* on the USS *Maine,* at the Battle of the Bulge.

It is here at Arlington that Memorial Day was instituted, first as Decoration Day, a time for "the strewing of flowers." The official proclamation read: "Let no neglect, no ravages of time, testify to the present or to the coming generations that we have forgotten as a people the cost of a free and undivided Republic. . . . Let us . . . garland the passionless mounds . . . with the choicest flowers of springtime; let us raise . . . the dear old flag they saved." Each Memorial Day weekend an army of the present-day generation descends and marks each of the almost quarter million tombstones with the Stars and Stripes. When that army returns to retire the flags, the cemetery is awash in bloom.

Arlington itself is a quiet place, yet each day—sometimes many times a day—the peace and solitude are broken. Guns fire a final salute. A lone bugler plays "Taps." Prayers are raised up. Good-byes are said. Each time the sounds punctuate the fogs of January, there is a new stone. Each time spring dogwoods shiver at the shock of a rifle volley, there is a new stone. As the tide of summer tourists streams in from the Visitor Center at the entrance to the cemetery, then ebbs and flows along the meandering paths, the caissons roll through and leave a wake of fresh stones. When fall leaves turn scarlet and winter snows begin to fall, they blanket more stones. And every day, the sacrifices the nation has endured to secure justice and become one people are written again in stone.

A walk among Arlington's stones is a journey of personal memories. The *Apollo* astronauts who died. A young president, John Fitzgerald Kennedy, and a Mississippi-born civil rights leader, Medgar Wiley Evers, both assassinated in 1963. Battles remembered vividly by those who were there or dimly from radio broadcasts by those who kept the home fires burning during World War II or Korea's darkest days. Stories told by old soldiers. Books or movies about heroes black, white, red, brown, and yellow. Here, a name that rings a bell for those old enough to recall Vietnam: General Creighton Williams Abrams Jr.; there, a boy of only twenty-one who died in a Mekong Delta rice paddy far away from home.

"Here rests in honored glory an American soldier known but to God," reads another stone, one that stands in proxy for all the lost and unidentified dead of the wars of the twentieth century and is guarded day and night. The Tomb of the Unknowns is where our country's presidents come to honor all who have served and died in war, and where foreign heads of states lay wreaths in recognition of America's role in winning peace. Each half hour in summer—and each hour October 1 through March 31—the guard is changed as four million visitors a year record the scene.

Some stones are large and grand and boast of long, impressive military careers; others merely hint. Major General John Lincoln Clem put on his tomb just his year of birth, 1851, and that of his death, 1937, and only one battle of more perhaps than even he could count. He was "the drummer boy of Chicamauga," a nine-year-old orphan—the youngest ever U.S. Army soldier—who volunteered to drum the 22nd Michigan Infantry into that epic Civil War battle. He served fifty-three more years.

Here wives may share their military husbands' final honor. Journalist Marguerite Higgins, whose heroic coverage from the front in the earliest days of the Korean War made her nationally famous, and the silver screen's Constance Bennett rest here because their husbands served the nation. Jacqueline Bouvier Kennedy Onassis lies here, too, alongside the martyred thirty-fifth president, their infant Patrick, and an unnamed daughter, who died at birth. Nearby is Bobby, the other Kennedy brother who was gunned down.

More and more it is women's own military service that earns them hallowed ground. "My Sweet Little Wife, Whose Beauty Could Only Be Outlived by My Love . . ." reads the somber head-high stone of Major

Marie Therese Rossi. "The First Woman Combat Commander to Fly into Battle," her sunny, confident smile, broadcast on the evening news in the early days of the Persian Gulf War, won America's heart. "This is the moment . . . I've trained for," she reassured the world. Five nights later she was dead. Her Army Chinook helicopter had hit an unlit tower. All aboard were killed.

The tombstones celebrate heroes, the Audie Murphies, as well as ordinary men and women who also did the job of war, brought peace home, and went back to live their lives as plain old John or Jane Q. Citizen. "When we assumed the soldier," Washington said of his fledgling nation's first troops, "we did not lay aside the citizen."

Under Arlington's stones lie three of the six marines who raised the flag at Iwo Jima. Arizona Pima Indian Ira Hayes, New Hampshire mill worker Rene Gagnon, and their sergeant, Michael Strank, one of nearly seven thousand who soon would die taking Mount Suribachi, are remembered for the hope and fortitude they gave to their country via one news-flashed image of fighting men and Old Glory.

Other stones speak famous names: Private (only later a Supreme Court Justice) William O. Douglas, Joe "The Brown Bomber" Louis, Army Tech 3 Samuel D. (for Dashiell) Hammett. Their names became far better known for what they did after guns went silent, yet as their tombstones attest, each would boast in death that he had once been one of Uncle Sam's GIs.

The stone marking the grave of the oldest—or longest deceased—soldier at Arlington, John Green, commander of a company of Minute Men, is in Section 1, along with nine other patriots of the Revolution, all reinterred here from older cemeteries. Near their stones, the tablelike monument of Washington's architect, Pierre Charles L'Enfant, in Section 2, diplays his original concept for the city that lies beyond this site.

To wander among these stones is to experience four hundred years of American history. Captain John Smith journeyed up the Potomac from Jamestown, noting small Algonquin settlements along these shores in 1608. A half century later, Virginia's royal governor gave the fertile land to a sea captain as payment for transporting settlers here; the sea captain promptly traded it for six hogsheads of tobacco and thought he had got the bargain. During the American Revolution, eleven hundred acres passed into Washington's family when his stepson and aide, John Parke Custis, purchased the land, dreaming of settling his young family here after the war. But after witnessing Lord

Cornwallis and the British surrender at Yorktown, John succumbed to a fever that was rampant in the Yankee camp, and the land passed to his infant son, George Washington Custis.

In 1824, when the Revolutionary hero Lafayette returned in triumph to the country he had helped wrest from British hands, he made a point to journey here to reminisce about that war. By then, Arlington House, Washington Custis's vast, hilltop plantation house with its classical columns and impressive portico, already was a landmark. When Custis's only child, Mary, wed a promising young West Pointer in the mansion's parlor on June 30, 1831, it was the social event of the Washington season. Their wedding date still is celebrated each year for tourists, with the bride's wedding finery laid out upon the beds and cookies and lemonade prepared for guests. That her soldier groom was Robert E. Lee was fateful; their marriage would make Arlington necropolis to the nation.

On April 18, 1861, on the brink of the Civil War, President Abraham Lincoln offered Lee command of the new Union Army. Virginia had not yet joined the Confederacy, but it was inevitable, and with sadness Lee, who was no slave owner, declined. He later wrote to his sister, "With all my devotion to the Union and the feeling of loyalty and duty as an American citizen, I [am not able] . . . to raise my hand against my relatives, my children, my home. . . ."

In May, Union troops crossed the Potomac and took up positions around the Lee-Custis mansion. By the time the land was officially declared a Union cemetery in 1864, more than a dozen Union dead already had been buried here. Private William Christman, Company G, 67th Pennsylvania Infantry, a twenty-one-year-old

farm boy and fresh recruit, was the first casualty. His grave lies with other Civil War graves in Section 27 near the cemetery's northern boundary.

The Tomb of the Unknown Dead from the Civil War marks what had been a grisly pit for all that could be found of some 2,111 "Johnny Rebs" and Union soldiers killed at Bull Run. It was dug in Mary Lee's cherished rose garden on orders of a grieving Union general whose soldier son was killed by Southern guerillas. By war's end, a sea of plain wooden crosses (later replaced with stones) marked Arlington. General Lee never saw them. Mrs. Lee returned just once, but refused to leave her carriage.

WALLACE D
MOORE
LTC
US ARMY
KOREA
VIETNAM
MAR 15 1929

ALVIN
PHILLIP
KATZ
SGT
US ARMY
KOREA
MAY 8 1930
MAY 22 1999

GEORGE F
VAUGHAN
LCDR
US NAVY
VIETNAM
MAY 18 1931
FEB 24 2000

No matter what the beliefs of those who sacrificed for their nation, a secure place is theirs at Arlington. All faiths are welcome here, as the rows of stones attest. The various Christian crosses—including those of the Presbyterian, United Methodist, Russian Orthodox, Lutheran, Episcopal, and Greek faiths—are well represented on the tombstones. The Hebrew Star of David, the Mormon Angel Moroni, the Muslim crescent and star, and the Buddhist Wheel of Righteousness appear frequently, along with the emblems of the Unitarian, the Konko-Kyo and many other faiths. Atheists too are welcome, and their tombstones display a distinctive atom-like symbol. Arlington opens her arms to all her heroes and heroines.

There is a symbolic line that begins at the base of the Lincoln Memorial on the Washington side of the Memorial Bridge—itself a literal link—that is meant to reunite North and South after a war one military leader called "the chastening of the nation, to make it see its destiny when it would not." The axis extends across the Potomac, marches up the center of Memorial Drive, is briefly visible in darker stones in the floor of the Women's Memorial at Arlington's ceremonial entrance, continues on up the hill past the Kennedy Eternal Flame, and ends at a memorial for Robert E. Lee at Arlington House.

There is another symbolic linkage in the line. The living democracy that thrives across the bridge in L'Enfant's city owes its vigor and its soul to the generations of the brave men and women who gave their lives to make it so. The future of the nation has been secured and will continue to be made safe by those who rest and will someday come to rest in this place. We are free because they served and died. That is the message of Arlington National Cemetery. It is the nation's story carved in stone.

—Linda Witt
Women In Military Service For America Memorial Foundation

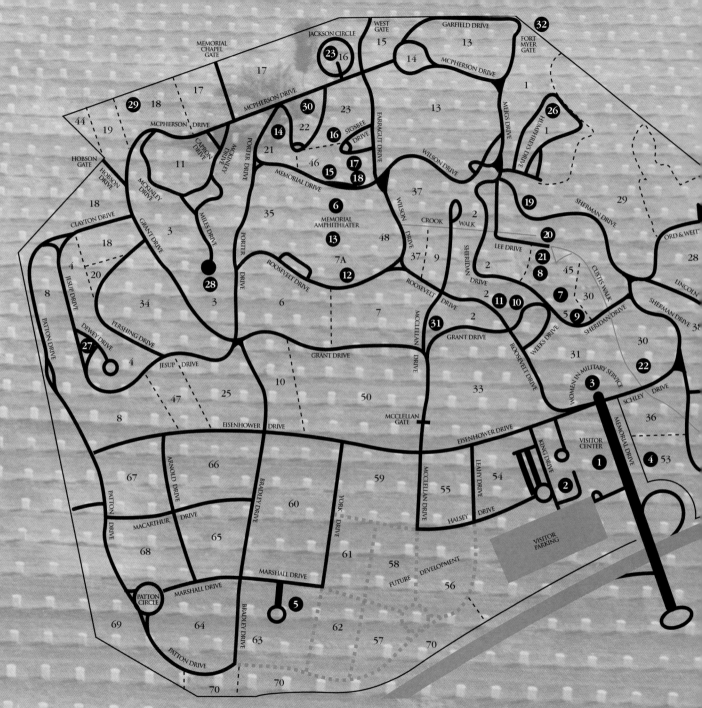

POINTS OF INTEREST

See Index page 93 for information about and location of stones in this book.

Circled numbers on the map indicate the following points of interest:

1. Visitor Center

2. Administration Building

3. Women In Military Service For America Memorial, honoring the women who served from the American Revolution through today

4. Seabees Memorial

5. Columbarium

6. Memorial Amphitheater

7. The Kennedy Eternal Flame

8. Robert F. Kennedy—President John F. Kennedy's brother—Attorney General and Senator

9. Oliver Wendell Holmes Jr., Civil War veteran and Supreme Court Justice

10. Daniel "Chappie" James Jr., first African American four-star general, United States Air Force

11. Admiral Robert Edwin Peary, polar explorer and Medal of Honor winner, and, nearby, his North Pole codiscoverer Matthew Henson

12. Joe Louis (Barrow), world heavyweight champion boxer, World War II veteran

13. Tomb of the Unknowns

14. Nurses Memorial

15. Audie Murphy, most decorated World War II soldier

16. Mast of the USS *Maine,* sunk in Havana Harbor

17. Memorial to the crew of the Space Shuttle *Challenger*

18. Iran Rescue Mission Memorial for servicemen killed in hostage rescue attempt

19. Tomb of the Unknown Civil War Dead

20. Arlington House, restored memorial to Confederate General Robert E. Lee

21. Pierre Charles L'Enfant, designer of the capital city, reinterred here in 1909

22. William Howard Taft, President and Chief Justice, the only other president besides Kennedy buried at Arlington

23. Confederate Monument, marking a section for burial of Confederate soldiers

24. Section 27, dedicated to U.S. Colored Troops and residents of Freedman's Village

25. Iwo Jima Memorial (the United States Marine Corps Memorial)

26. Dr. Anita Newcomb McGee, founder of Army Nurse Corps

27. U.S. Coast Guard Monument

28. Miles Mausoleum

29. World War II Argonne Cross

30. Rough Riders Monument

31. Chaplains Monument

32. Fort Myer Chapel

MEMORIAL DAY

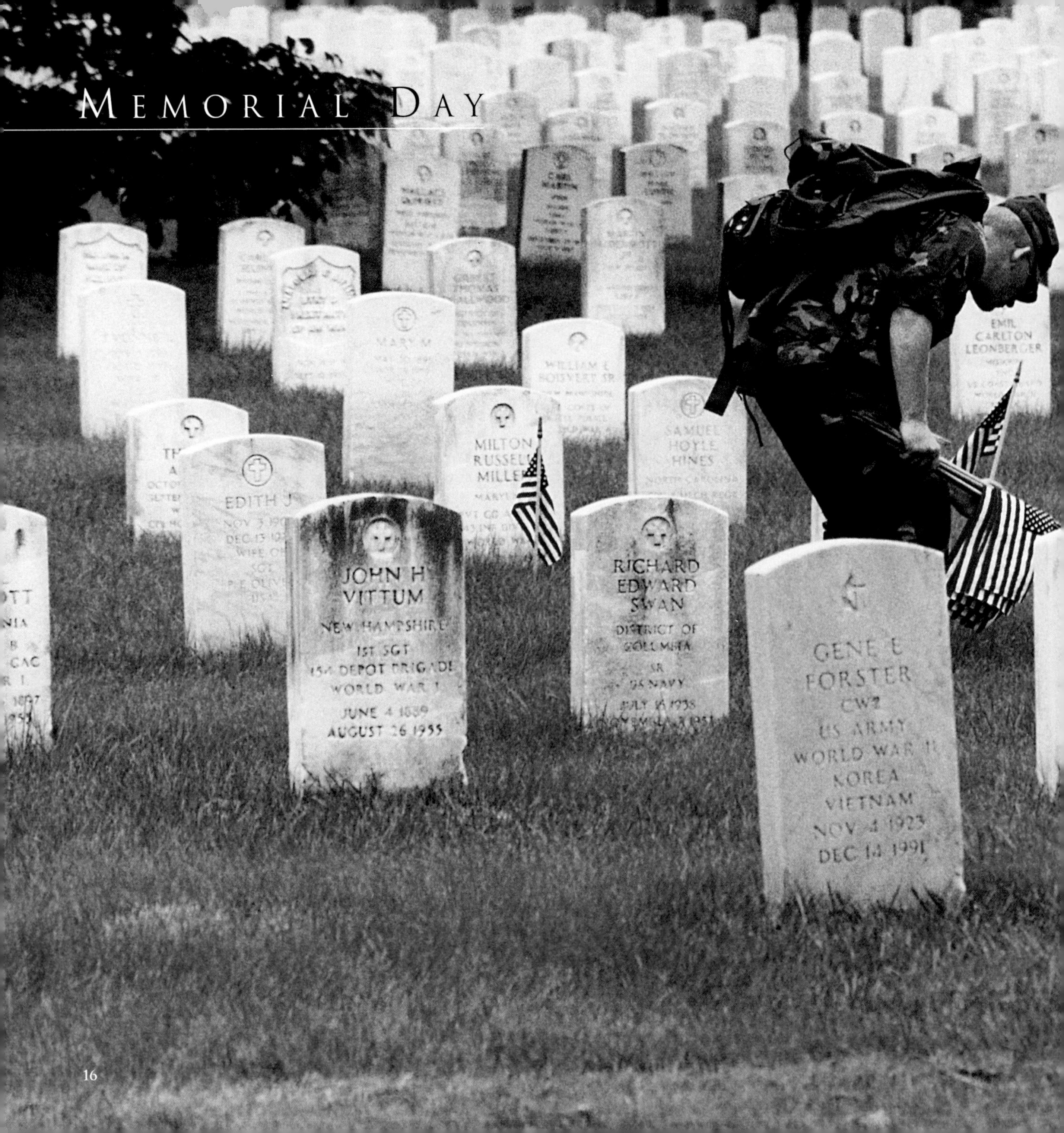

Arlington National Cemetery is a confounding place. How can such a tourist draw teeming with people be so calm? How can such somber hallowed ground feel so uplifting and welcoming? Bright blue and red tour buses wind their way up sinuous streets named Eisenhower, MacArthur, Marshall, Patton, Sheridan, Sherman, Grant, and Roosevelt, each name, like a carillon, pealing out a piece of history. American tourists—from Iowa and Georgia, Texas and Maine—wander through the grounds, clad in the universal garb of jeans or shorts, T-shirts emblazoned with the names of sports teams, and athletic shoes manufactured in steamy places in Asia where the GI Joes and Janes of World War II were probably deployed. The visitors study maps or focus cameras and politely help a Japanese or German tourist find the signs to John F. Kennedy's grave and Eternal Flame. The teams of honor guards, each in full dress uniform for one of the two dozen daily funerals, contrast sharply with this casually dressed civilian throng. The guards dazzle children with their spit-shined elegance, and simply by their presence, these young men and women in the uniform of their country reinforce the message that these silent rows of graves convey: Liberty is not a given, but a nation's constant goal. Peace always has a price, and the evidence that the price was paid—and may come due again—is here.

Tomb of the Unknowns

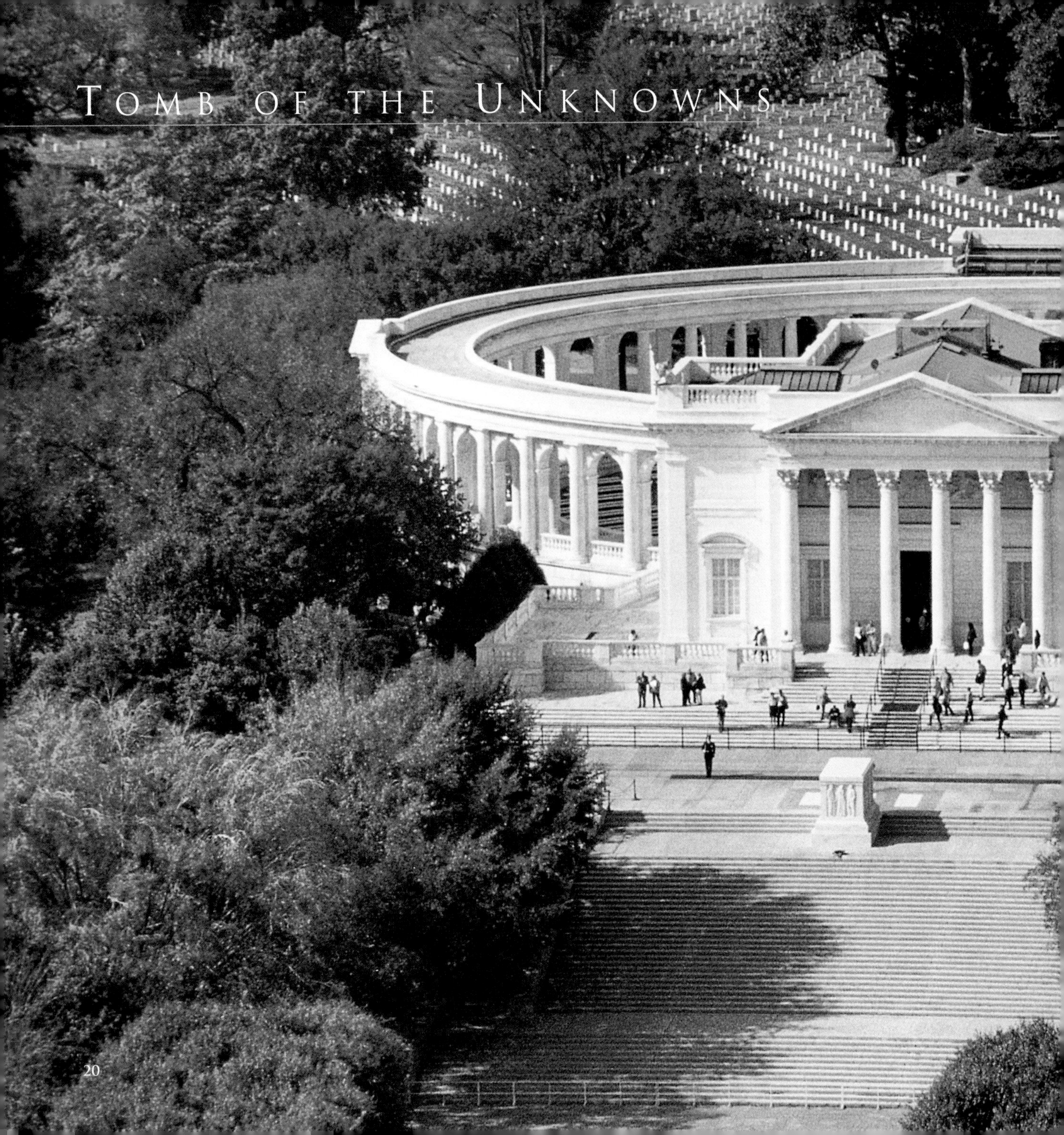

No part of Arlington evokes the terrible price war demands more than the Tomb of the Unknowns. A World War I "Dough Boy" drew the duty of choosing the first of the three Americans "known only to God" who would rest here. Battle-scarred and highly decorated, Sgt. Ed Younger gazed at four identical caskets brought from French battlefields where 1,237 unidentified Americans were buried. Each coffin held the remains of a once-starry-eyed young man who fought "the Great War to end all wars." Younger laid a white rose on one soldier's bier. "Something . . . pulled me. A voice seemed to say, 'This is a pal of yours.'"

Before an identical tomb for one of the 87,411 unknown dead and missing in World War II could be built, the Korean War erupted; it left 9,037 unidentified dead by the time of its cease fire. Congress decided to bring one unknown soldier from each of these two wars to rest together "in honored glory" beside the sarcophagus of the soldier from World War I.

The remains of a fourth unknown soldier, from the Vietnam War, were subsequently identified through DNA; his remains were taken home by his Missouri family. Thus, medical technology may have ended the "unknowns" tradition, but one wonders how many old soldiers of generations hence will visit this solemn place and hear a voice that says, "This is a pal of yours."

21

On Veterans' Day in 1961, John Fitzgerald Kennedy made the first of his presidential visits to Arlington, but he was no stranger here. Many friends from his World War II Navy *PT-109* days are buried here. Once—on an impromptu spring visit—he walked up to Arlington House, gazed at the city beyond, and remarked how peaceful it was: "I could stay here forever." After JFK's assassination, Jacqueline Bouvier Kennedy, perhaps remembering his love of the place, chose this spot for the graves of her husband and their two dead infants and personally lighted the Eternal Flame. Family members selected the Massachusetts granite slabs, interplanted with sedum and fescue, to re-create the New England fields in which JFK played as a child. The whole world watched as the slain president was laid to rest November 25, 1963. Twenty-three other Americans, who also had served their country, were buried at Arlington National Cemetery that day, each with equal dignity and protocol. The president's widow was buried here in 1994; his brother, Senator Robert Kennedy, in 1968.

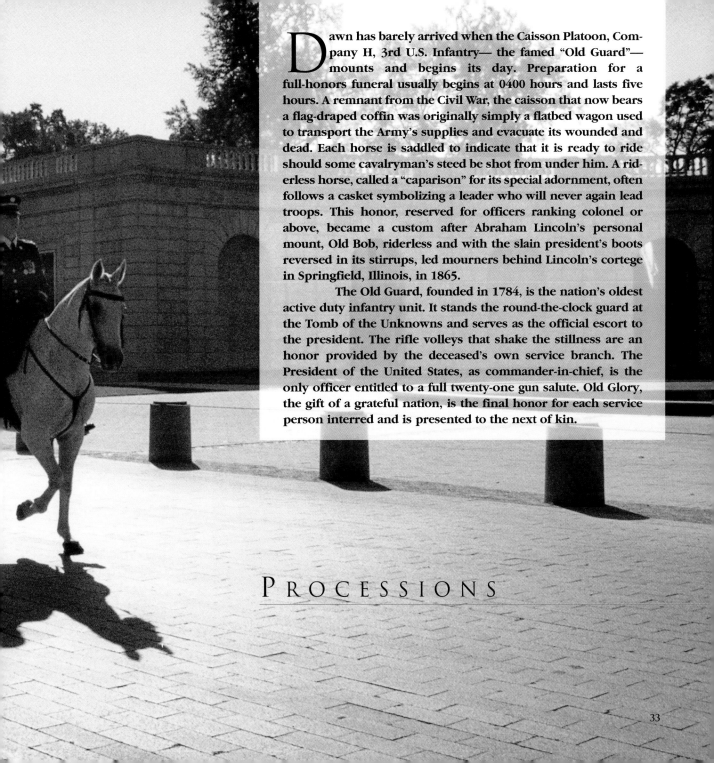

Dawn has barely arrived when the Caisson Platoon, Company H, 3rd U.S. Infantry— the famed "Old Guard"— mounts and begins its day. Preparation for a full-honors funeral usually begins at 0400 hours and lasts five hours. A remnant from the Civil War, the caisson that now bears a flag-draped coffin was originally simply a flatbed wagon used to transport the Army's supplies and evacuate its wounded and dead. Each horse is saddled to indicate that it is ready to ride should some cavalryman's steed be shot from under him. A riderless horse, called a "caparison" for its special adornment, often follows a casket symbolizing a leader who will never again lead troops. This honor, reserved for officers ranking colonel or above, became a custom after Abraham Lincoln's personal mount, Old Bob, riderless and with the slain president's boots reversed in its stirrups, led mourners behind Lincoln's cortege in Springfield, Illinois, in 1865.

The Old Guard, founded in 1784, is the nation's oldest active duty infantry unit. It stands the round-the-clock guard at the Tomb of the Unknowns and serves as the official escort to the president. The rifle volleys that shake the stillness are an honor provided by the deceased's own service branch. The President of the United States, as commander-in-chief, is the only officer entitled to a full twenty-one gun salute. Old Glory, the gift of a grateful nation, is the final honor for each service person interred and is presented to the next of kin.

PROCESSIONS

The Nurses Memorial, honoring Spanish-American War and World War I nurses, was rededicated in 1971 to all military nurses. To Arlington visitors, it is also a reminder that American women have always stood by their flag and countrymen. Jemima Warner, this country's first woman killed in action, died December 11, 1775, in the Pennsylvania Rifle Battalion's attack on Quebec. After menfolk left to fight the Revolutionary War, wives and daughters took up arms, nursed wounded, spied on enemy lines, and faced danger—even hanging had King George's forces won—simply by protecting their farms and homes. "Destroy all the men in America and we shall still have all we can do to defeat the women," an awed British officer told Lord Cornwallis. Some women disguised themselves as men to fight—and won soldier's pensions from the grateful infant nation for their effort. Other patriot women took up guns or cannon ramming staff and fought in skirts—only to be remembered by one name: Molly Pitcher. Even more often, women served as nurses.

The U.S. military also has always counted on and honored the contributions of servicemen's wives, and at Arlington they share their husband's gravesites. However, a new era began in World War I, when the Navy secretary learned that law did not require his yeomen to be male and, for the first time, enlisted 12,000 yeoman (F)—or females. By World War II, recruiting posters boasted that "Woman's Place in War" was in every military branch "to free a man to fight"; some 400,000 did. Today, America's women serve alongside their brothers, comprising roughly 14 percent of personnel, and a nation has learned to honor warrior daughters as it does its warrior sons.

Women at Arlington

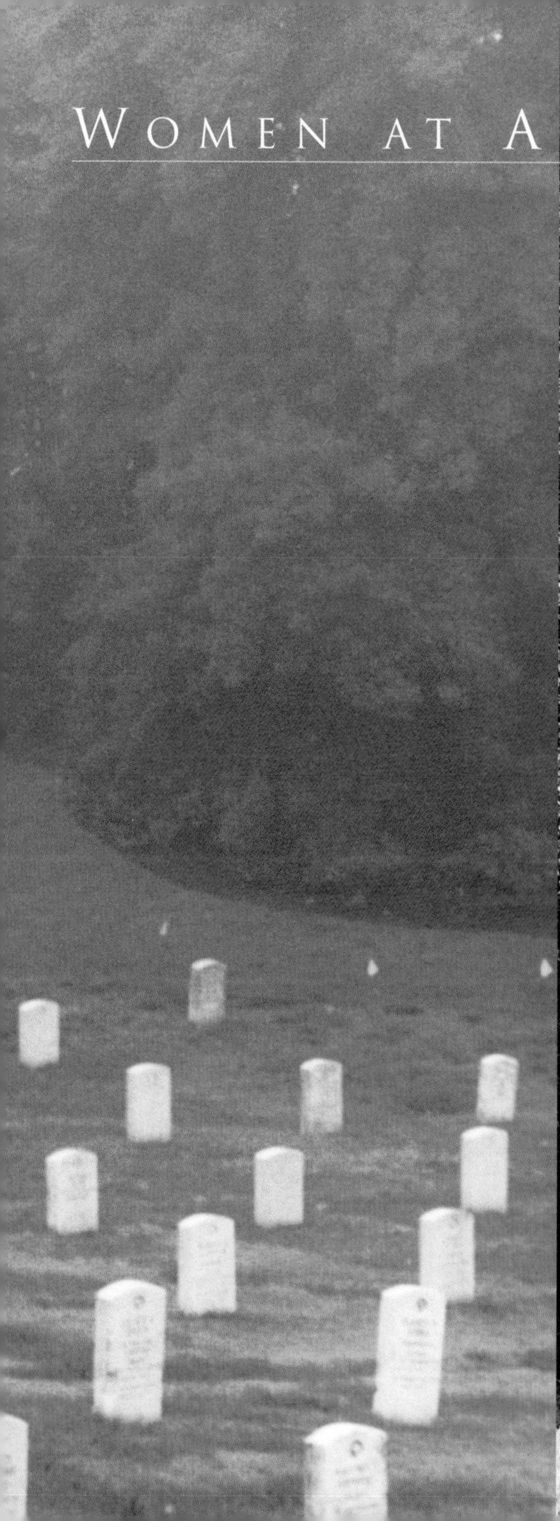

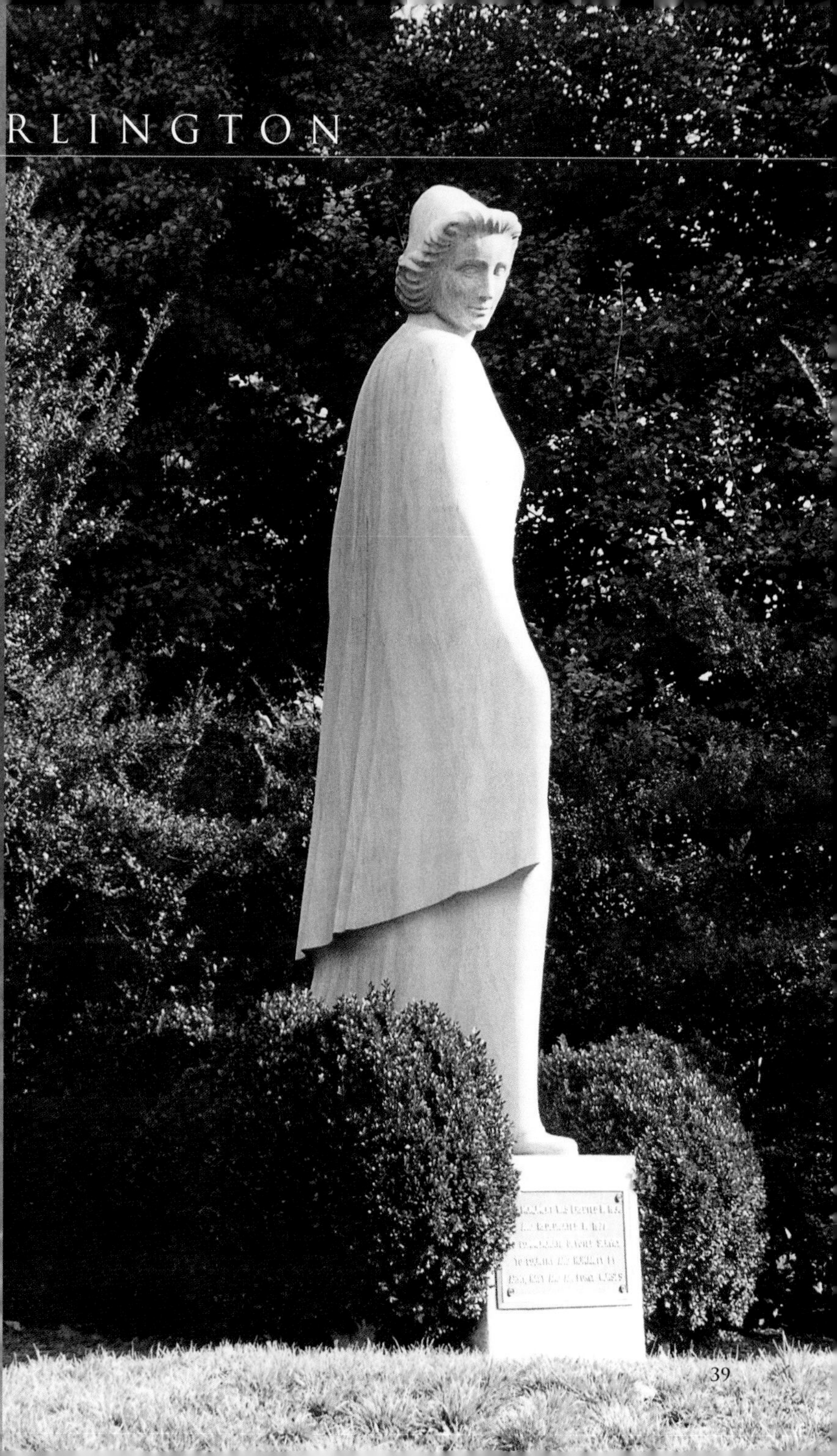

JANE A. DELANO
BORN MONTOUR FALLS, N.Y., MARCH 12, 1862
DIED SAVENAY, FRANCE, APRIL 15, 1919
FAITHFUL UNTO DEATH

ELIZABETH G. LEE
NURSE
1870 —— 1927

CITATION NOV. 2, 1918
HEROIC CONDUCT
WHILE ATTACHED EVACUATION
HOSPITAL No. 4
MEUSE—ARGONNE OFFENSIVE

526-B
ANITA N. McGEE
ACTG.
ASST. SURG.
U.S. ARMY
SP. AM. WAR

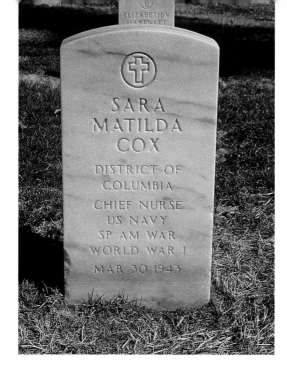

SARA
MATILDA
COX

DISTRICT OF
COLUMBIA

CHIEF NURSE
US NAVY
SP AM WAR
WORLD WAR I
MAR 30 1943

GRACE M
HOPPER
RADM
US NAVY
WORLD WAR II
KOREA
VIETNAM
DEC 9 1906
JAN 1 1992

JULIET ANN
OPIE
HOPKINS
MAY 7 1818
MAR 9 1890

ETHEL R
THOMPSON
MASSACHUSETTS
NURSE
ARMY NURSE CORPS
WORLD WAR I
FEBRUARY 5 1885
MARCH 6 1951

41

MARIE THERESE ROSSI
MAJOR
UNITED STATES ARMY
JANUARY 3, 1959 ~ MARCH 1, 1991

FIRST FEMALE COMBAT COMMANDER
TO FLY INTO BATTLE

OPERATION DESERT STORM

*In Memory Of My Sweet Little Wife, Whose Beauty
Could Only Be Outlived By My Love For Her.*

For African Americans, Arlington is especially hallowed ground. The American Revolution set whites free; the Civil War, as Abraham Lincoln promised at Gettysburg, would "resolve . . . that this nation shall have a new birth of freedom." The Civil War was black Americans' war, and when it was declared, thousands of fugitive slaves fled "to the Army." While the North fought to preserve the Union and the South fought to preserve property and states' rights, the black man and woman fought for far less abstract reasons: to reunite families, to win their own liberty. More than 180,000 African American troops served in our Union forces, and the tombs of those buried in Arlington—including three Medal of Honor recipients—are marked with the Civil War Shield and the letters "U.S.C.T.", indicating "U.S. Colored Troops." Many of the "contrabands"— slaves freed as the Union troops moved South—came here to work for the Army, settling here in a now unmarked and nearly forgotten "Freedman's Village," on the land that had once been a slave-worked plantation. Some 3,800 freedmen are buried in Arlington in tombstones marked simply "Civilian" or "Citizen."

MEMORIALS

L ong after the battlefields are green again, long after great warriors' stories fade from living memory, Arlington's stones will still
bear witness to memorable events and courageous fighters. Iwo
Jima, a mere eight square miles of Pacific volcano, taken at a cost of
nearly a thousand Marines per mile, was one such an epic moment
and group of men. The Battle of the Bulge, forty days of hell that sacrificed 77,000 Allied lives but routed the Germans and turned the tide
in Europe, was yet another. A simple cross recalls World War I's
Argonne—a hilly, woody, and, before it ended in November 1918, a
very bloody place in France—the stage on which "the Yanks" played
out the final scene of the war that decimated a generation. One stone
here recalls the frontier cavalry's Buffalo Soldiers, near legendary bat-
tle-seasoned black troops who gave backbone to Teddy Roosevelt's
impetuous charge up San Juan Hill. More mute testimony to that short
but strategic war: the reclaimed mast of the USS *Maine* (see page 54),
the U.S. Navy battleship whose sinking in 1898 in Havana Harbor
resulted in a loss of 260 sailors and launched the Spanish-American
War. Silent homage to the beginnings of another war: the stone com-
memorating those who died in 1964 when the USS *Forrestal* was
bombed in Vietnam's Gulf of Tonkin. Astronauts and Minute Men, Civil
War "boys in gray" and "boys in blue," military women and Native
Americans—each special memorial is a mirror to our past and the
nation we have become.

DEDICATED TO THE GALLANT AND VICTORIOUS
MEN AND WOMEN WHO PARTICIPATED IN THE
BATTLE OF THE BULGE, WORLD WAR II, 16
DECEMBER 1944 THRU 25 JANUARY 1945 IN
BELGIUM AND LUXEMBOURG. THE GREATEST
BATTLE EVER FOUGHT BY THE UNITED STATES
ARMY. PRESENTED BY THE VETERANS OF THE
BATTLE OF BULGE ON 16 DECEMBER 1986.

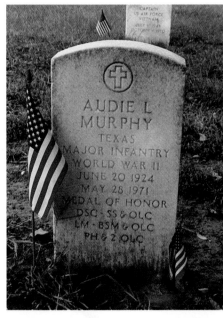

AUDIE L
MURPHY
TEXAS
MAJOR INFANTRY
WORLD WAR II
JUNE 20 1924
MAY 28 1971
MEDAL OF HONOR
DSC · SS & OLC
LM · BSM & OLC
PH & 2 OLC

GREGORY
PAPPY
BOYINGTON
MEDAL OF HONOR
COL
US MARINE CORPS
WORLD WAR II
DEC 4 1912
JAN 11 1988

JAMES H
DOOLITTLE
MEDAL OF HONOR
GEN
US AIR FORCE
WORLD WAR II
KOREA
DEC 14 1896
SEP 27 1993

THE MIGHTY EIGHTH
1942 1945
AIR FORCE
IN MEMORY OF THE 350,000
AIRMEN WHO SERVED
AND
IN MEMORY OF THE 47,742
COMBAT CREWMEN
KILLED OR MISSING
WHO PAID THE SUPREME SACRIFICE

U.S.S. CANBERRA CA-70

THIS MEMORIAL IS IN COMMEMORATION OF THOSE
WHO GAVE THEIR LIVES FOR THEIR COUNTRY WHEN
THE U.S.S. CANBERRA WAS TORPEDOED WHILE
OPERATING IN BATTLE AGAINST JAPANESE AIRCRAFT
OFF THE COAST OF FORMOSA ON OCTOBER 13, 1944

DEDICATED SEPTEMBER 18, 1999

THIS MEMORIAL PRESENTED TO ARLINGTON NATIONAL CEMETERY
BY THE U.S.S. CANBERRA ASSOCIATION AND ITS MEMBERS OF THE CREW

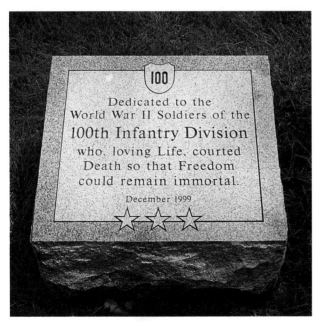

100
Dedicated to the
World War II Soldiers of the
100th Infantry Division
who, loving Life, courted
Death so that Freedom
could remain immortal.

December 1999

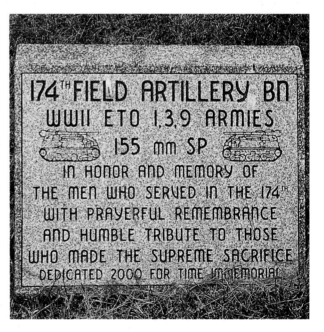

174TH FIELD ARTILLERY BN
WWII ETO 1,3,9 ARMIES
155 mm SP
IN HONOR AND MEMORY OF
THE MEN WHO SERVED IN THE 174TH
WITH PRAYERFUL REMEMBRANCE
AND HUMBLE TRIBUTE TO THOSE
WHO MADE THE SUPREME SACRIFICE
DEDICATED 2000 FOR TIME IMMEMORIAL

~ CAN DO

CULT WE DO AT ONCE; THE IMPOSSIBLE TAKES A BIT

IN MEMORY OF OUR MEN IN FRANCE
1917   1918

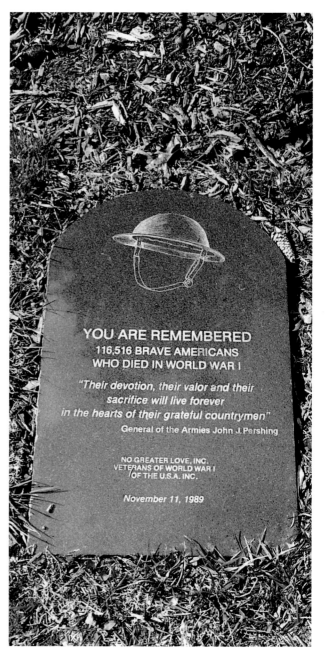

YOU ARE REMEMBERED
116,516 BRAVE AMERICANS
WHO DIED IN WORLD WAR I

"Their devotion, their valor and their
sacrifice will live forever
in the hearts of their grateful countrymen"
General of the Armies John J. Pershing

NO GREATER LOVE, INC.
VETERANS OF WORLD WAR I
OF THE U.S.A. INC.

November 11, 1989

BUFFALO SOLDIERS
CENTENNIAL CEREMONY
JULY 1, 1898 - JULY 1, 1998

DEDICATED TO THE BUFFALO SOLDIERS, 9th AND 10th
CAVALRY, AND THE 24th AND 25th INFANTRY REGIMENTS
(COLORED TROOPS) FOR VALIANT SERVICE IN THE
SPANISH-AMERICAN WAR. THEY CHARGED UP SAN JUAN
HEIGHTS AND EL CANEY, CUBA WITH TEDDY ROOSEVELT
AND THE ROUGH RIDERS.

IN MEMORY OF
THE WOMEN WHO GAVE THEIR LIVES
AS ARMY NURSES IN 1898
—
ERECTED BY
THE SOCIETY OF
SPANISH AMERICAN WAR NURSES

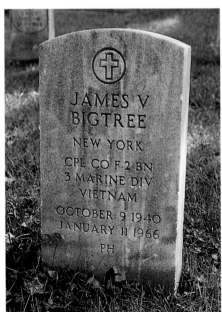

DIED IN FIRE AND EXPLOSIONS ✠ USS FORRESTAL JULY 29 1967

PR2 MARVIN J ADKINS	LT DENNIS M BARTON	AEAN ROBERT J DAVIES
WEST VIRGINIA	IOWA	ILLINOIS
JULY 28 1934	JANUARY 15 1935	NOVEMBER 21 1947
ADJ3 EDWARD R DORSEY	AE1 WALTER T EADS	AME1 JOHN J FIEDLER
CONNECTICUT	NEW ZEALAND	WISCONSIN
JUNE 30 1947	AUGUST 24 1937	AUGUST 24 1934
AMS3 RUSSELL L FIKE	AN JOHNNIE L FRAZIER	ADRAN RALPH E MANNING
PENNSYLVANIA	TEXAS	ALABAMA
NOVEMBER 27 1947	JULY 3 1947	SEPTEMBER 12 1947
AE3 LEROY MOSER	AMHC RICHARD L OWENS	AMH2 ERNEST E POLSTON
SOUTH DAKOTA	CALIFORNIA	SOUTH CAROLINA
AUGUST 27 1944	MAY 11 1929	MARCH 10 1936
ATR3 JOHN M PRUNER	AME2 DALE R ROSS	AMS2 JOHN F SNOW
MICHIGAN	MISSOURI	NEW YORK
MAY 14 1948	APRIL 23 1947	SEPTEMBER 10 1938
SN NELSON E SPITLER	LCDR GERRY L STARK	AN HAROLD D WATKINS
OHIO	NEBRASKA	KENTUCKY
JULY 2 1946	DECEMBER 23 1929	JULY 16 1945

GULF OF TONKIN VIETNAM

U S NAVY

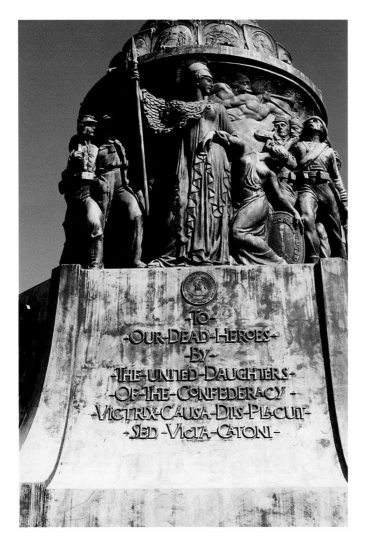

TO
OUR DEAD HEROES
BY
THE UNITED DAUGHTERS
OF THE CONFEDERACY
VICTRIX CAUSA DIIS PLACUIT
SED VICTA CATONI

JAMES RICHMOND
MEDAL OF HONOR
CO F
8 OHIO INF

JUN 3 1864

1861 5

CAPT. DAN'L M.
KEYS.
INDEPENDENT
WEST VA.
RANGERS.

NOTABLE STONES

Arlington resonates with the history every schoolchild learns, but even the most notable people remembered here lived lives whose layers the textbooks do not plumb. Washington's great architect, Pierre L'Enfant, who was asked to create a city "magnificent enough to grace a great nation" from swamp and wilderness, died penniless in 1825. Thanks to belated recognition of his genius and a special act of Congress, he was reinterred here in 1909. General "Black Jack" Pershing's career took him from America's frontier days (he fought the Apache and led the famous Sioux scouts) to its global era (in Cuba in 1898 fighting Spain, on Mexico's border in early 1900 chasing Pancho Villa, in Europe during World War I leading American forces to victory). Yet his personal life was so tragic: his wife and daughters died in a San Francisco fire while he was at war, and one grandson, whose matching simple stone stands near his, died in Vietnam.

West Pointer Abner Doubleday, a hero at Gettysburg, is far more famous for creating baseball—though historians now doubt that he did. Rear Admiral Robert Edwin Peary's epic quarter-century battle to locate the North Pole in 1909 made him the legend and cost him his toes; now—since 1988—his African American fellow explorer for twenty-two of those years, Matthew Henson, shares credit for codiscovery. A ship's cabin boy at twelve, Henson's nearby tombstone quotes the promise he made to Peary: "I will find a way or make one." Captain Robert Todd Lincoln, General-in-Chief U.S. Grant's aide and the only one of Lincoln's sons to reach adulthood, witnessed Union victory and Lee's surrender at Appomatox, but later bore the pain of committing his grief-mad mother to an asylum.

So well known yet so very human, the notable men and women here at Arlington personify "the better angels of our nature." The words are Lincoln's, from his inaugural address as he faced the threat to his beloved nation.

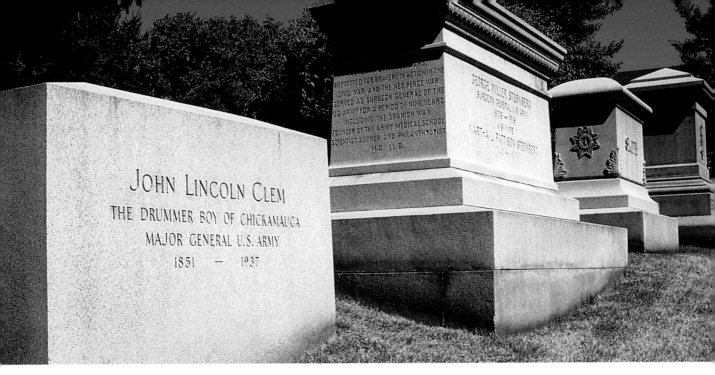

JOHN LINCOLN CLEM
THE DRUMMER BOY OF CHICKAMAUGA
MAJOR GENERAL U.S. ARMY
1851 — 1937

BREVETTED FOR BRAVERY IN ACTION IN THE
CIVIL WAR AND THE NEZ PERCE WAR.
SERVED AS SURGEON GENERAL OF THE
U.S. ARMY FOR A PERIOD OF NINE YEARS.
INCLUDING THE SPANISH WAR.
FOUNDER OF THE ARMY MEDICAL SCHOOL.
SCIENTIST, AUTHOR AND PHILANTHROPIST.
M.D. LL.D.

GEORGE MILLER STERNBERG
SURGEON GENERAL U.S. ARMY
1893 — 1902
HIS WIFE
MARTHA L. PATTISON STERNBERG
1849 — 1919

JOHN J
PERSHING
MISSOURI
GENERAL OF
THE ARMIES
OF THE
UNITED STATES
SEPTEMBER 13 1860
JULY 15 1948

RICHARD W
PERSHING
NEW YORK
2LT
US ARMY
VIETNAM
OCT 25 1942
FEB 17 1968

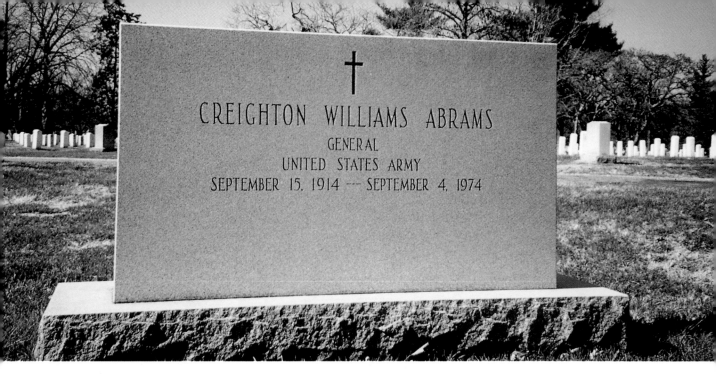

CREIGHTON WILLIAMS ABRAMS
GENERAL
UNITED STATES ARMY
SEPTEMBER 15, 1914 --- SEPTEMBER 4, 1974

SAMUEL D
HAMMETT
MARYLAND
TEC3 HQ CO
ALASKAN DEPT
WORLD WAR I & II
MAY 27 1894
JANUARY 10 1961

MEDGAR W
EVERS
MISSISSIPPI
TEC 5
QMC
WORLD WAR II
JUL 2 1925
JUN 12 1963

ROBERT TODD
LINCOLN

Here among the quarter-million stones one poet called "the bivouac of the dead," Nature has a way of easing grief and loss. In spring, she tempers winter's heavy air and lightens saddened hearts with frisky zephyr breezes that dance with visitors' umbrellas and redden children's noses. The Eternal Flame breathes on, the tourists come and go, the guard at the Tomb of the Unknowns presents arms, salutes, and performs its changes routinely, and wave upon wave of spring blossoms burst upon the scene, reminding us again that life indeed goes on. When Washington's famous cherry trees begin to bloom, and just before the dogwood and azaleas flower, Arlington's tulips raise their fresh green leaves to the sky and flex waxy petals in the first warm sun. Just by repeating this predictable seasonal pattern, spring provides solace for a mourner's soul.

Summer follows, bringing sun-dappled mornings and lingering afternoons that welcome quiet walks in the shade of ancient oaks. Families come to bury or visit their dead. Rains nurture the grass, which in turn wipes the rawness from the recent graves. In fall, vividly colored leaves softly drift around the stones and settle in for winter. Near Christmas, a sea of red bows and wreaths brightens the last short, cold days, until finally the snow or winter fog rings down the curtain on another year. And still the Unknowns' guard is changing.

RAYMOND
ORVIN
FLETCHER

EDITH M

INDEX

Page numbers are indicated in **boldface.**

Abrams, Creighton Williams, General, USA, commander in the Vietnam War and later Army Chief-of-Staff. Section 21. **65**

Argonne Cross, commemorates epic World War I battle. Section 18 near McPherson Drive. **52**

Arlington House (Lee-Custis Mansion). At the top of Custis Walk between Sheridan and Sherman Drives. **11, 19, 75, 82–83**

Auld, Hugh, veteran of the American Revolution. Section 2, Grave 4801. **59**

Battle of the Bulge Memorial, dedicated to the memory of the 77,000 Allied World War II casualties. Section 46. **48**

Bigtree, James V., Corporal, USMC Vietnam War. Section 37, Grave 4222. **56**

Birchfield, Marie Axcie, Spanish-American War Army nurse, who shares a tombstone with her mother, Ella M. Gillen, Army Nurse Corps. Section 21, Grave 15990. **88**

Boyington, Gregory "Pappy," Colonel, USMC, World War II founder of the "Black Sheep" squadron, Medal of Honor and Navy Cross winner, prisoner of war, Section 7A, Grave 150. **48**

Brown W. U. T., U.S.C.T ("Colored Troops"). Section 13, Grave 14393. **45**

Buffalo Soldiers Centennial Ceremony Memorial. Section 22, McPherson Drive. **53**

Bussey, Cyrus, Major General, 3rd Iowa Calvary, Civil War Union Army. Section 3, Grave 1466 on McKinley Drive. **71**

Chaffee, Roger Bruce, Lieutenant Commander, USN, and astronaut, died in the *Apollo One* command module disaster. Section 3, Grave 2502-F. **60**

Challenger Memorial. Commemorates the seven astronauts who died aboard the Space Shuttle *Challenger*. Section 46, near the Memorial Amphitheater. **60**

Christman, Claude B., Corporal, Spanish-American War Army, died in the Battle of Manila in the Philippines. Section 22, Grave 15350. **70**

Clem, John Lincoln, Civil War Union Army Drummer Boy of Chickamauga, Spanish-American War veteran, retired as a Major General. Section 2, Grave 993. **64**

Columbarium, Section 63, near the corner of Marshall and York Drives. **19**

Confederate Memorial. Section 16, Jackson Circle off McPherson Drive. **58, 85**

Cox, Sara Matilda, Spanish-American War Army nurse, World War I Chief of the Navy Nurse Corps. Section 21, Grave 2114. **41**

Delano, Jane A., American Red Cross Nursing Service chair and second superintendent of the Army Nurse Corps, nicknamed "the General" or "Sister Jane" by War Department colleagues, died in France during World War I. Section 21, Grave 6. **40**

Doolitte, James H., Lieutenant General, USAF, World War I aviator, world record test pilot, led the "Toyko Raid" (the first hit back at Japan in World War II), Medal of Honor winner. Section 7A, Grave 110. **48**

Doubleday, Abner, Major General, Civil War Union Army. Section 1, Grave 61. **67**

Douglas, William O., Private, USA, World War II, Associate Justice, U.S. Supreme Court. Section 5, Grave 7004-B-1. (There are six other Supreme Court justices who are buried nearby: Oliver Wendall Holmes, Jr., Potter Stewart, William Brennan, Thurgood Marshall, Harry Blackmun, and Warren Burger.) **66**

Eighth Air Force Memorial. Section 34 on Grant Drive. **49**

Eternal Flame. At the gravesite of President John F. Kennedy, directly above the Women In Military Service For America Memorial between Sheridan and Sherman Drives. **28–29, 30, 92**
See also Kennedy gravesite.

Evers, Medgar W., Tech Sargeant, Quarter Master Corps, USA, World War II, and African American civil rights leader. Section 36, Grave 1431. **65**

Gagnon, Rene, Corporal, USMC, one of the six Marines who raised the Stars and Stripes on Iwo Jima's Mount Suribachi, World War II. Section 51, Grave 543. **46**

Gillen, Ella M., Spanish-American War Army nurse, who shares a tombstone with her daughter, Marie Axcie Birchfield, Army Nurse Corps. Section 21, Grave 15990. **88**

Green, John, Colonel, American Revolution, Tenth Virginia Volunteers. Section 1, Grave 503. **59**

Grissom, Virgil, Lieutenant Colonel, USAF, and astronaut, died in the *Apollo One* command module disaster. Section 3, Grave 2503-F. **60**

Hammett, Samuel D. (Dashell), Sargeant, USA World Wars I and II, writer and Pinkerton detective; buried at Arlington with honors appropriate to rank over the objections of FBI Director J. Edgar Hoover, who opposed his leftist politics. Section 343, Grave S-19. **65**

Harris, James H., Sergeant and Medal of Honor winner, U.S.C.T ("Colored Troops"). Section 27, Grave 985-H. **45**

Hayes, Ira Hamilton, Corporal, USMC, one of the six Marines who raised the American flag atop Iwo Jima's Mount Suribachi, World War II. Section 34, Grave 479-A. **46**

Henson, Matthew, Arctic explorer and codiscoverer of the North Pole. Section 8, Grave S-15, near codiscoverer Admiral Robert Edwin Peary's memorial (a large globe, with a bronze star marking the North Pole). **67**

Higgins, Marguerite, Pulitzer Prize-winning Korean War correspondent, who also won the U.S. Army's campaign ribbon for her participation in the surrender of German soldier prisoners, and the wife of Lieutenant General William Hall, USAF. Section 2, Grave 4705B. **43**

Hopkins, Juliet Ann Opie, the Civil War's "Florence Nightingale of the South," wounded at Battle of Seven Pines. Hopkins was originally buried in her son-in-law general's gravesite; her tomb was not marked until 1987. Section 1, Grave 12. **41**

Hopper, Grace Murray, Rear Admiral, USN, and computer pioneer. Section 59, Grave 973. **41**

Hoxie, Richard L., Brigadier General, USA, and husband of Vinnie Ream Hoxie, the sculptor who created the Abraham Lincoln statue in the Rotunda of the United States capitol and the figure of Admiral David D. Farragut that stands in the square bearing his name in Washington, D.C. Section 3, Grave 1876. **70**

Iwo Jima Memorial. *See* United States Marine Corps Memorial.

Jarvis, Gregory B., astronaut and civilian payload specialist who researched the design of liquid-fueled rockets for the National Aeronautics and Space Administration. Section 46. **60** *See Challenger* Memorial.

Katz, Alvin Phillip, Sargeant, USA, Korean War, Purple Heart winner. Section 65, Grave 3498. **13**

Kennedy gravesite, for President John F. Kennedy, wife Jacqueline Bouvier Kennedy Onassis, infant son Patrick, and an unnamed infant daughter. Below the Eternal Flame. **28–29, 30, 92**

Kennedy, Robert Frances, U.S. Senator and Attorney General. To the left of the Kennedy gravesite, below Arlington House. **31, 82**

Keys, Daniel M, Captain, Civil War, Independent West Virginia Rangers. Section 13, Grave 13615. **58**

Lee, Elizabeth C. World War I Army Nurse Corps, cited for Heroic Conduct during the Meuse-Argonne Offensive, the final epic battle with which World War I was won. Section 21, Grave 13. **40**

L'Enfant, Pierre, Brevet Major, American Revolution, and planner of the Federal City of Washington, D.C. Section 2, Grave 3. **62–63**

Lincoln, Robert Todd, Captain, Civil War Union Army. Son of President Abraham Lincoln. Section 2, Grave 13. **69**

Louis, Joe, Tech Sergeant, USA, World War II, Legion of Merit winner, and boxing's heavyweight Champion of the World. Section 7A, Grave 177. **67**

McAuliffe, Christa, astronaut selected from among more than 11,000 teacher applicants to become the first educator in space, killed when the Space Shuttle *Challenger* exploded on launch. Section 46. **60** *See Challenger* Memorial.

McCain, John Sidney Jr., Admiral, USN. As Commander in Chief of the Pacific Command he had command of all U.S. forces in Vietnam when his son, now Senator John McCain, became a POW inmate of the notorious Hanoi Hilton. Section 3, Grave 4001-A. **6**

McCain, John Sidney Sr., Admiral, USN, World War II. Annopolis-trained admiral for whom the naval destroyer USS *John S. McCain* was named, and his wife, Katherine V. McCain. The grandfather of the current U.S. Senator John McCain, Admiral McCain Sr. was profiled in the 1943 *Current Biography* as "one of the Navy's best plain and fancy cussers." His West Point-educated

brother, Brigader General William Alexander McCain, who had chased Poncho Villa with General Pershing, is buried next to him. Section 3, Grave 4356. **6**

McClellan Arch. The cemetery's main gate. Constructed in the 1870s in tribute to Civil War General George B. McClellan. He is not buried at Arlington. **75**

McClurg, Walter A., Medical Director of the U.S. Navy and his wife, Edmonia Mason McClurg, who was also the widow of Lieutenant Commander Theodosius B. Mason, USN. Section 1, Grave 403-A. **43**

McGee, Anita Newcomb, Army physician and founder of the Army Nurse Corps, veteran of the Spanish-American and Russo-Japanese Wars. Section 1, Grave 526-B. **40**

McKee, Thomas Hudson, lst Lieutenant Volunteer Infantry, Civil War Union Army. Section 1 on Humphreys Drive. **71**

McNair, Ronald E., astronaut and mission specialist, Ph.D. in quantum electronics and laser technology and the second African American astronaut, researched electro-optic laser modulation for satellite-to-satellite space communications. Killed in the explosion of Space Shuttle *Challenger*. Section 46. **60** *See Challenger* Memorial.

Marshall, Thurgood, Associate Justice, U.S. Supreme Court, Section 5, Grave 40-3. (Six other Supreme Court justices are buried nearby: Oliver Wendall Holmes, Jr., Potter Stewart, William Brennan, William O. Douglas, Harry Blackmun, and Warren Burger.) **66**

Mason, Theodosius B., Lieutenant Commander, USN, shares a tombstone with his widow, Edmonia, and her subsequent husband, Medical Director of the U.S. Navy Walter A. McClurg. Section 1, Grave 403. **43**

Meigs, Montgomery, General, Union Army Quartermaster, with wife Louisa, and in the separate tomb (foreground) with the slain "boy in blue" atop, the Meigs' son, Lieutenant John Rodgers Meigs, whose death prompted Meigs to appropriate Arlington as a federal cemetery. Section 1, Grave 1. **43**

Memorial Amphitheater ("America's Temple of Patriotism") and Tomb of the Unknowns. On Memorial Drive between Porter and Wilson Drives. **20–27, 89**

Mills, Benjamin, U.S.C.T ("Colored Troops"). Section 13, Grave 16571. **45**

Moore, Wallace D., Lieutenant Commander, USA, Korea and Vietnam Wars. His tombstone is marked with the Buddhist Wheel of Righteousness. Section 67, Grave 1636. **13**

Morningstar, Robert Lee, Staff Sergeant, USMC. Section 12, Grave 4612. **56**

Murphy, Audie, Major, USA Infantry, Medal of Honor Winner and World War II's most highly decorated soldier. Section 46, Grave 366-11. **48**

Nurses Memorial, heroic size Frances Rich sculpture dedicated to Army and Navy nurses. Section 21 (called the "Nurses Section," although some nurses are buried elsewhere in the cemetery). **38–39, 88**

100th Infantry Division Memorial. Section 34 on Grant Drive. **49**

174th Artillery Battalion Memorial. Section 34 on Grant Drive. **49**

Onizuka, Ellison S., Lieutenant Colonel, USAF, astronaut mission specialist killed when the Space Shuttle *Challenger* exploded on launch. Section 46. **60** *See Challenger* memorial.

Peary, Robert Edwin, Admiral, USN, leader of the polar expedition that discovered the North Pole, April 6, 1909. Section 8, Grave 6-15, near codiscoverer Matthew Henson's black granite memorial. **67**

Pershing, John J., the second General of the Armies (his predecessor was General George Washington). Section 34, Grave S-19. **64**

Pershing, Richard Warren, 2nd Lieutenant, USA, Vietnam era, killed in action. Section 34, Grave S-19, next to his grandfather, John J. Pershing. **64**

Reynolds, Frank, Staff Sergeant, USA, and veteran broadcaster. Section 7A, Grave 180. **67**

Resnik, Judith A., astronaut and mission specialist, Ph.D. in electrical engineering and expert in neurophysiology. Killed in the Space Shuttle *Challenger* explosion. Section 46. **60**
See Challenger Memorial.

Revolutionary Soldiers Memorial, Section 1, Grave 4501. **59**

Rice, Edmund, Civil War, Medal of Honor winner at Gettysburg. Section 3, Grave 1875. **68**

Richmond, James, Medal of Honor winner, Eighth Ohio Infantry, Civil War. Section 27, Grave 886. **58**

Rinehart, Stanley Marshall, Major, USA, and physician, and his wife, World War I war correspondent and mystery author, Mary Roberts Rinehart. Section 3, Grave 4269. **43**

Roosa, Stuart Allen, Lieutenant Colonel, USAF, and astronaut, *Apollo 14*. Section 7A, Grave 73. **60**

Rossi, Marie Therese, Major, USA, and helicopter pilot, Persian Gulf War casualty. Section 8, Grave 9872. **42**

Scobee, F. R. "Dick," Lieutenant Colonel, USAF, Vietnam combat veteran, Commander Space Shuttle *Challenger,* killed when the shuttle exploded on launch. Section 46, Grave 1129-3. **60**

Seabees Memorial. Memorial Drive. **50–51**

Smith Michael J., Commander, USN, and astronaut, killed when the Space Shuttle *Challenger* exploded on launch. Section 46. **60**
See Challenger Memorial.

Spanish-American War Nurse Memorial. Section 21 on McPherson Drive at Lawton Drive. **53**

Strank, Michael, Sergeant, USMC, died in the assault on Iwo Jima's Mount Suribachi after the famous flag-raising episode; the photograph of the event became the model for the United States Marine Corps Memorial. Section 12, Grave 7179. **46**

Thompson, Ethel R., World War I Army Nurse Corps. Section 21, Grave 2112-1. **41**

Tomb of the Unknown Dead of the War of 1812. The remains of these fourteen servicemen were discovered in 1905 by construction workers at the Washington Navy Yard and reinterred in Arlington later that year. Section 1, Grave 298. **10**

Tomb of the Unknowns. *See* Memorial Amphitheater.

U.S.C.T. (United States "Colored Troops"), African American former slaves who fought for the Union during the Civil War, some buried anonymously. Includes three Medal of Honor winners. Section 13. (This area also includes many former slave civilians—"unknown" and "citizen"—who worked for the Union Army and lived in Freedman's Village, which was located here during the Civil War.) **44**

United States Coast Guard Memorial. Section 4 where Jesup and Dewey Drives meet. **55**

United Staters Marine Corps Memorial (Iwo Jima statue), based on an April 1945, news photograph by Associate Press cameraman Joe Rosenthal; commemorates that turning point of the war in the Pacific during which an unprecedented 27 Medals of Honor were awarded, as well as other Marine Corps engagements throughout history. At the end of Custis Walk, beyond the Ord and Wetzel (east) Gates. **46–47**

USS *Canberra* Memorial. Section 34 on Roosevelt Drive. **49**

USS *Forrestal* Memorial. Section 46. **57**

USS *Maine* Memorial. Section 24 on Sigsbee Drive. **54**

Vaughan, George F., Lieutenant Commander, USN, Vietnam. His tombstone indicates the Angel Moroni of the Mormon faith. Section 46, Grave 1176. **12**

Viet-Nam Era (Indian Warrior) Veterans Memorial. Section 8 on Patton Drive. **56**

Wainwright, Jonathan Mayhew, General, USA, World War II, Japanese POW and Medal of Honor winner, and his wife, Adele Holley Wainright. General Wainwright was in command when Bataan Peninsula fell to the Japanese. Section 1, Grave 358-B. **43**

Warren, Earl, 1st Lieutenant, USA, World War II, later California governor, 1952 presidential candidate, and Chief Justice of U.S. Supreme Court. Section 21, Grave S-32. **66**

Women In Military Service For America Memorial. At the end of Memorial Drive on the symbolic line linking the Abraham Lincoln Memorial and the Robert E. Lee Memorial at Arlington House. **61, 74**

World War I Memorial. Section 34 next to General of the Armies John J. Pershings's grave, off Pershing Drive. **52**